neutral
essentials

with **Alex Anderson**

7 Quilt Projects • 3 Keys to Fabric Confidence • Fat-Quarter Friendly

     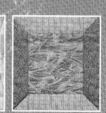

C&T PUBLISHING

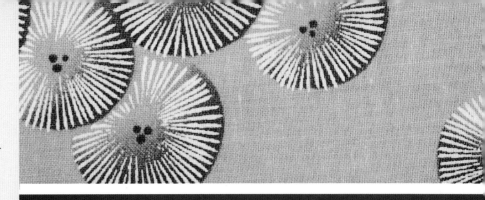

Text copyright © 2007 Alex Anderson

Artwork copyright © 2007 C&T Publishing, Inc.

Publisher: Amy Marson

Editorial Director: Gailen Runge

Acquisitions Editor: Jan Grigsby

Editor: Liz Aneloski

Technical Editors: Teresa Stroin and Nanette S. Zeller

Copyeditor/Proofreader: Wordfirm Inc.

Cover Designer/Design Director: Kristy K. Zacharias

Junior Designer: Kerry Graham

Illustrators: Josh Mulks and Tim Manibusan

Production Coordinator: Tim Manibusan

Photography: Luke Mulks and Diane Pedersen,
unless otherwise noted

Published by C&T Publishing, Inc., P.O. Box 1456,
Lafayette, CA 94549

Library of Congress Cataloging-in-Publication Data
Anderson, Alex.
  Neutral essentials with Alex Anderson : 7 quilt
projects, 3 keys to fabric confidence, fat-quarter
friendly.
      p. cm.
  ISBN-13: 978-1-57120-418-9 (paper trade : alk. paper)
  ISBN-10: 1-57120-418-0 (paper trade : alk. paper)
  1. Quilting–Patterns. 2. Patchwork–Patterns. I. Title.

TT835.A493672 2007
746.46'041–dc22

2007003876
Printed in China

10 9 8 7 6 5 4 3 2

dedication

To my dear quilting friends, who make working and playing
in this industry pure joy. When I'm asked, "What is the best
part of quilting?" the answer is, unequivocally, "You."

acknowledgments

Thank you to

P&B Textiles and Robert Kaufman, for graciously providing
wonderful fabric to play with.

Olfa, for great tools to work with.

Bernina, for letting me create and play with their terrific
sewing machines.

Bob and Heather Purcell of Superior Threads, for their
excellent product and for their dedication to educating the
consumer about the wonderful world of thread.

Darra Williamson, for being my guiding light.

Erica von Holtz, for her eagle eye.

And a special thanks to

**Mary Kay Davis, Pam Vieira, Cheryl Uribe, Paula Reid,
Dee Christopher, and Darra Williamson**, for lending their
creativity and quilting talents to the creation of this book.

contents

introduction

Several years ago—more than I care to count—I attended a one-day seminar at Empty Spools quilt shop in Alamo, California. Sadly, that wonderful shop is no longer around, but on that particular day, we were charmed by the energy and humor of noted quilt-maker and author Mary Ellen Hopkins. Midway through her trunk show, Mary Ellen jumped on her soapbox to proclaim the absolute necessity of rounding out our fabric stashes with a healthy dollop of neutral fabrics. Her philosophy was twofold: she believed that a well-rounded stash just can't have enough of these versatile pieces and that there just aren't many really good ones out there from season to season.

Eager quilter that I was, I took Mary Ellen's message to heart—and the quest began. As a result of her powerful suggestion, I began to purchase neutral fabrics that previously might not have come home with me, and they seemed to accumulate with astonishing speed! My stash of neutral fabrics was taking serious form.

Not long after, while sitting in church one bright and sunny Sunday morning, I was tapped on the shoulder by my friend Deanna. Deanna was excited that she was going to be a first-time grandma and chose that moment to ask that I make a quilt for the baby. I've got to be honest—at that time, I was still feeling a *tiny bit* selfish about giving away my quilts. I did not exactly jump with joy at her request. But, wouldn't you know it, the sermon that day was about sharing. Needless to say, I agreed to make the quilt.

Deanna was fairly specific about what she wanted. Her plans included an embroidered Spanish prayer, and I envisioned trumpeting angels. Then I had one of those glorious ah-ha! moments. The neutral fabrics I had been collecting and hoarding would make the perfect background for this quilt. I dug into my ever growing stash and began to cut and randomly piece the neutral background together. Before long, the quilt was completed, and I was totally hooked on using neutral fabric. In fact, I made a slightly modified version of that quilt to keep for my family.

I quickly planned my next neutral quilt, with visions of stars and pinwheels dancing in my head. Diana McClun, who was writing her first book—*Quilts! Quilts!! Quilts!!!*—with Laura Nownes, saw the quilt taking form on my sewing room wall and asked if it could be included in their book. (The quilt debuted on page 6 of that book, and now you can see it again—along with the complete instructions to make it—on page 40 of this book.) My mini group asked me to teach a class on working with neutrals, and, as they say, the rest is history.

To this day, I have not tired of making quilts with a neutral palette, and my stash of neutral fabrics continues to grow. Over the years, as I have made and shared these quilts, I've discovered that people respond strongly to them. Thus came the idea of writing this book, and I was excited when C&T agreed to publish it. The possibilities for using these fabrics are endless, and with just a few tips and guidelines, I guarantee you smashing results.

Along with sharing some of my favorites, I called upon a group of extraordinary quilters to lend their talents to create a collection of quilts to add to mine. We gathered for a day at my house and swapped ideas and fabrics, and then each quilter put her personal spin on a quilt made with neutral fabrics. I knew the projects were in more-than-capable hands, but I wasn't sure what to expect. Would all the quilts look the same, or would each one make it on its own?

As the quilts found their way to my door, it immediately became clear not only that each quilt sang but that together they sang the "Hallelujah Chorus"! Although all were made from a neutral palette, each had a unique personality. From visually striking graphic designs to designs with the delicacy of a frosted wedding cake, the quilts knocked my socks off—so much so, that I had to make another one! Once you see them, I bet you'll need to make one too.

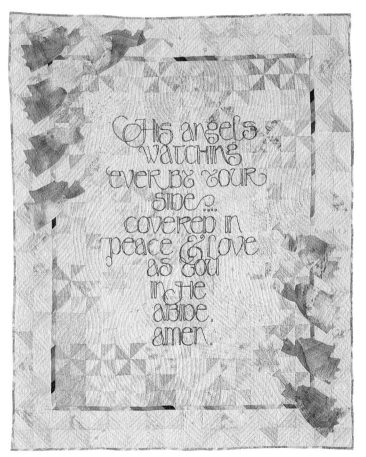

Angel Quilt

working with neutrals

Over the years, I have probably made a dozen quilts using only white, beige, tan, gray, and other "noncolored" prints. After months of making quilts in a wide variety of colored fabrics, I welcome the opportunity to clear my visual palette by creating a quilt entirely with neutrals. I think of these quilts as the intermezzo course in my usual brightly colored fabric diet. Invariably, I love the results, and before long, I find myself reaching once again for my ever growing stash of these subtle—but oh-so-inspiring!—fabrics.

Making a quilt entirely from neutral fabrics is not much different from making a quilt in any other color scheme. Just keep a few simple "rules" in mind, and I guarantee you'll be making smashing neutral quilts in no time flat!

what is a neutral?

Webster's New World Dictionary defines "neutral" as "having little or no decided color; not vivid" and "free from mixture of other colors." You'll find this definition—or one much like it—in just about any English-language dictionary, and the definition translates perfectly to the neutral fabrics you'll find in your favorite quilt shop. Neutrals include a wide range of white, off-white, cream, ecru, beige, tan, and even gray fabrics. Within this range, you'll find a sizable variety in character of print, from tiny florals to bold stripes to large-scale paisleys. I was lucky to be introduced to neutrals early in my quiltmaking experience and to be trained to check them out whenever the opportunity presented itself. That's the secret: recognizing the versatility of these wonderful fabrics and buying them when you see them.

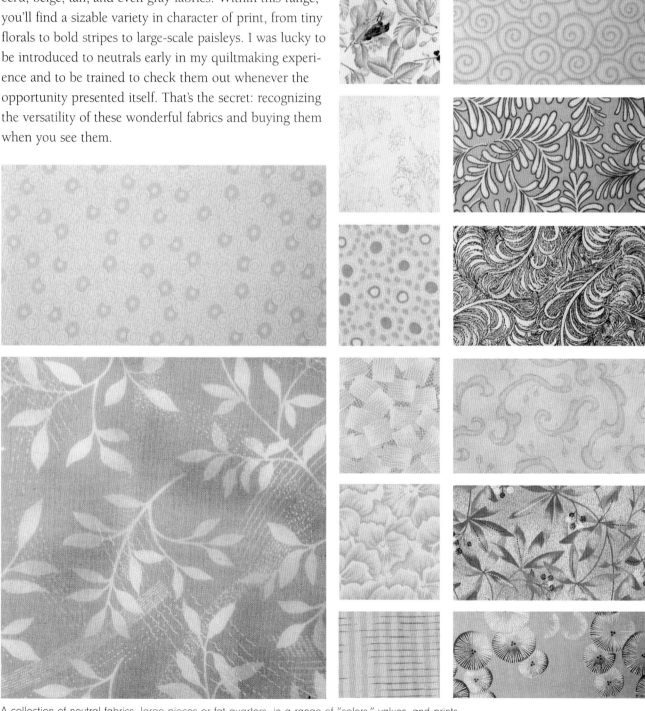

A collection of neutral fabrics—large pieces or fat quarters—in a range of "colors," values, and prints

the three keys to success

There are three key elements to consider in choosing fabrics for quilts: color, value, and character of print. Let's look at these elements one at a time and see how neutrals play into this formula.

color

Do you know a single quilter who is not drawn to the rows of colorful bolts that call from the shelves of quilt shops and the booths of quilt show vendors? Let's face it, we're like little kids attracted to the vibrant colors in the candy shop window. The subtle neutral fabrics are easy to overlook in this dizzying display.

Big mistake! Those neutral fabrics can be lifesavers in a traditional, multicolored quilt, but that's only half the story. Quilts made *entirely* with neutral fabrics can be stop-in-your-tracks gorgeous. Furthermore, I've never known anyone who didn't love quilts made in this style, which makes neutral quilts ideal for gifts.

There are a couple things to remember when choosing the fabrics for a fabulous neutral quilt.

■ Always include a touch of white for sparkle. If you don't, the quilt will look muddy.

Muddy

Sparkle

■ Variety adds spice. Avoiding the tendency to be matchy-matchy is more important than ever in a neutral quilt. Mix white, cream, ecru, beige, tan, and even gray—the more the merrier. The neutral family is surprisingly large, and the element of mix and match will give your quilt richness and depth.

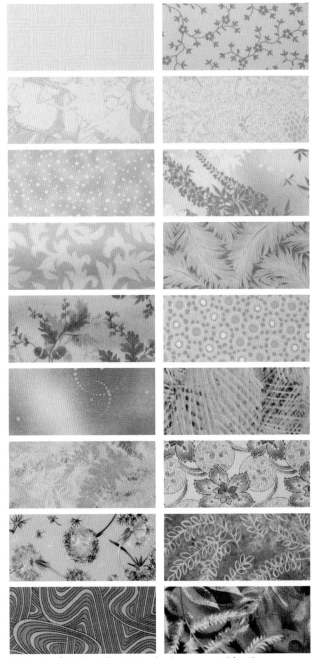

Swatches illustrating the large neutral family: white, ecru, beige, and so on

■ Call on bridge fabrics to help the various neutrals blend. A bridge fabric incorporates several members of a single color family—in this case, the neutral family—in one print.

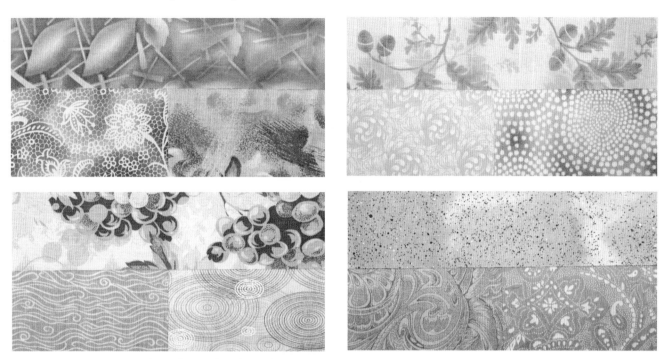

Several examples of varied neutrals and the bridge fabric that pulls them together

value

Value refers to the degree of lightness or darkness of the color in a particular fabric. Because the element of contrasting color is removed—or at least drastically minimized—when you are working with neutrals, value becomes even more important in helping you establish the design of your quilt. In fact, working exclusively with neutrals is an excellent way to learn and master the concept of light, medium, and dark.

Keep in mind that the value of a fabric is relative; that is, the value of a fabric depends upon the fabrics you surround it with. A fabric that reads as a light compared to one fabric may read as a dark when placed side-by-side with a lighter piece.

Three groups of three swatches each; one fabric appears progressively as the dark, the medium, and the light.

Differences in value—whether subtle or more pronounced—help create the contrast that defines the design of your quilt. The degree of contrast can give your quilt a distinctive look or feel.

For example, low contrast between the backgrounds and the pieced or appliquéd patterns can give your quilt an elegant and dreamy flavor. I used this look in my quilts *Stars and Pinwheels* (page 40) and *LeMoyne Star Appliqué Medallion* (page 18). To duplicate this look, limit the fabrics to the range from white to medium-value neutrals.

For a little more punch, push the medium-value neutrals darker, perhaps even into the lighter browns, as Cheryl Uribe did in her quilt *Paradox*. This quilt projects a dramatic, contemporary image due to the greater degree of contrast in the value of the fabrics. Cheryl enhanced this bolder look by using large blocks with simple shapes that create the illusion of secondary patterns.

Paradox, pieced and machine quilted by Cheryl Uribe, 2006

tip

Speaking of appliqué ... Although neutrals are traditionally viewed as the ideal background for classic appliqué, don't feel confined to a single neutral background. Many years ago, I met a woman who had made a classic, Elly Sienkiewicz-inspired Baltimore Album quilt. Rather than using a single white or off-white solid or subtle print for the background, this quilter created a pieced background of neutral fabrics as the backdrop for her intricate appliqué.

The subtly shifting values gave the quilt a shimmering effect, and the quilt was an absolute knockout.

character of print

Character of print—sometimes called visual texture—refers to the type, size, and scale of the printed motif on a particular fabric.

This is the element we quilters most often overlook as we aim to create a distinctive pattern in our quilts. Not good! Variety in character of print creates contrast just as variety in color and value can. The results may be a bit more subtle, but the distinction between the pattern and the background—or, say, between star points and star center—should be there. (If you squint and *can't* see contrast between the shapes, perhaps because a large flower at the tip of a star point is the same color as and blends into the background, try cutting the star point from a different part of the print, or switch to a different print altogether.)

Sawtooth Star block with little contrast in character of print

Sawtooth Star blocks with variety in character of print

When collecting neutrals—as with any other fabrics—look for variety in character and scale of print. Here are some examples of prints to look for:

■ Florals, vines, and other growing things

■ True geometrics, including plaids, stripes, and checks

■ Directionals (fabrics with motifs printed in a repeating, predictable one-way fashion)

■ Dots and circles

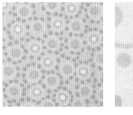 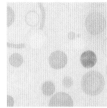 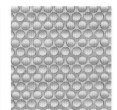

■ Paisleys and feathers

■ Tone-on-tone or other subtle prints

■ Prints with white (for sparkle)

tip

If you have a hard time determining the potential of a fabric with respect to character of print, cut a 2″ square opening in the center of a 3″ × 5″ index card and place the opening over various places on the print. This technique will give you a good idea of how the fabric will read when cut up and pieced or appliquéd in your quilt.

You don't need to be in love with every fabric in your quilt. Because neutrals tend to be subtle by nature, they offer a great opportunity to use quirky—or even questionable—prints you might never touch otherwise. One time, about twenty years ago, my eyes locked on what at the time seemed like a hideous, what-could-I-be-thinking neutral print. The beige background was printed with a combination of chunky white polka dots *and* clunky white stripes. For some reason, I brought it home. (As I recall, my friend Diana McClun *made* me buy it.) To my surprise, this ugly duckling turned out to be the most wonderful piece of fabric! I used it over and over in my scrappy neutral quilts, hoarding the tiniest pieces as I watched the yardage shrink. I think I actually cried—or at least whined loudly—when the last scrap was gone.

Postscript: In preparing the fabric sample for this book, guess what I found? Yippee!

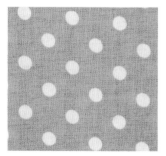 

Once you've got a good variety of prints to work with, mix them up in your quilt. Place stripes beside florals and polka dots beside paisleys. You'll be amazed at the richness this variety adds to the finished quilt, even when all the fabrics are from the same color family.

permission to stretch

If the idea of making a quilt from neutrals intrigues you, but you're unwilling to give up color completely, consider adding a touch of soft color (for example, pale pink or pale green) to the mix. Paula Reid used this approach with great success in her quilt *Make Mine Neapolitan*. The addition of a few pale, tone-on-tone pink prints adds to the romantic, feminine flavor of the quilt without compromising the overall neutral palette.

A wonderful bridge fabric (page 8) that incorporates the desired color can help you take this next step. Paula found just such a fabric in the lovely faded cottage-rose print she used as a border.

Make Mine Neapolitan, pieced and machine quilted by Paula Reid, 2006

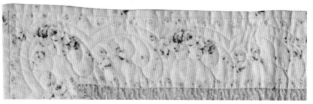

Border of *Make Mine Neapolitan*

building and caring for a neutral fabric collection

Because I find myself going back to neutrals over and over, I want to keep this part of my stash stocked. I find that neutral fabrics I purchased ten years ago blend seamlessly with other, newer neutrals. Unlike many other prints that are subject to the current trends of color and pattern, neutrals are timeless.

Building a stash of neutral fabrics takes time. The best advice I can give you is to buy them when you see them. Each season, look for interesting new ones to add to your collection.

There is one exception to my scoop-'em-up approach to collecting neutral prints. Periodically, a new crop of white-on-white prints will hit the marketplace. Many of these fabrics feature ditzy small-scale white motifs stamped on a white background. Unfortunately, the contrast is so subtle that when placed in a quilt, these fabrics all tend to read the same—that is, as solid white. Don't waste your energy collecting every new one that catches your eye. Keep a few reliable staples in your stash and periodically add one or two new ones with prints that are unusual or larger in scale.

Swatches of ditzy white-on-white prints, unusual, and larger-scale motifs

tip

If you are not sure how a small-scale or subtle print will read in your quilt, stand back from the fabric and squint at it. This technique will give you a good idea how the fabric will appear when cut up and used in the quilt.

When I purchase neutrals for no particular reason but to build my stash, I typically buy ⅓- to ½-yard cuts. When I run across a good potential bridge fabric (page 8), I buy *at least* ½ yard. As you begin to use these wonderful neutral and bridge fabrics, you'll develop a good sense of which to buy in smaller (for example, fat quarter) or larger amounts.

choosing and implementing a design

Over time, I have discovered that simple blocks make the best choices for a neutral palette. Keep in mind that simple doesn't need to mean boring. If you doubt this for a moment, just flip through the pages of this book to see the magic you can make with old favorites such as Log Cabin (page 29), Sister's Choice (page 13), Dresden Plate (page 24), and Spools (page 44).

Designs with a strong diagonal—for example, *Suzanne* (page 32) by Dee Christopher—give you lots of opportunity to play and experiment. Block combinations also work well. A Sawtooth Star, for example, looks the same from every angle. But pair it with the equally simple—and classic—Pinwheel, with its large half-square triangles and strong diagonal lines, and you've got an instant winner. I used this pairing to make *Stars and Pinwheels* (page 40). Although I made this quilt many years ago, it has never lost its appeal for me.

Use shifting values to create movement and visual excitement. See how the blades of the pinwheel seem to spin with just the slightest manipulation of value from blade to blade. Even the aforementioned traditionally static Sawtooth Star becomes "active" if you vary the values of the star points within the block. The eye will seek the repeating value and be drawn around the block to find it, creating the illusion of motion.

Pinwheel block with variation in value of the blades to suggest motion

Sawtooth Star block with star points alternating from light to medium to suggest motion

Another trick for adding visual interest with simple blocks is to combine them in varying sizes. Depending upon the basic grid, a 12″ block can be repeated as a 6″ block, a 4″ block, or a 3″ block.

Sample combining blocks in various sizes

Creative sets—for example, sets including filler strips and sashing or blocks turned on point—offer another means to add visual punch. Mary Kay Davis's quilt *Crème Brulée* (page 24) is a good example.

projects
with
neutrals

LeMoyne Star appliqué medallion

FINISHED QUILT SIZE 45½″ × 45½″

SKILL LEVEL Confident beginner

Pieced and machine appliquéd by Alex Anderson and machine quilted by Paula Reid, 2006

love antique quilts and draw great inspiration from them. *LeMoyne Star Appliqué Medallion* was inspired by a quilt made in 1880 that I found pictured in the book *America's Glorious Quilts*, edited by Dennis Duke and Deborah Harding (see Recommended Reading on page 54). The original quilt, from the private collection of Phyllis Haders, featured appliqués in reds, yellows, and greens on a white background. The arrangement was unusual and worked beautifully in neutrals, especially when I added several bridge fabrics to blend the beige and gray prints. I used a light, subtle print for the background so Paula could have fun with the quilting—and obviously she did!

materials

Fabric amounts are based on a 42″ fabric width.

- **Very light tone-on-tone cream print:** 2¼ yards for background and borders (**Fabric A**)

- **Light-medium beige print:** ⅜ yard for LeMoyne Star block and star center appliqués (**Fabric B**)

- **Light-medium beige and gray print:** ¾ yard for swag and star appliqués and flat piping (**Fabric C**)

- **Medium beige and gray print:** ⅞ yard for vines (**Fabric D**)

- **Assorted light, light-medium, medium, and medium-dark neutral prints:** ¾ yard *total* for leaf, small flower, small flower center, tulip center, and tulip appliqués*

- **Very light cream solid:** ⅜ yard for binding (**Fabric E**)

- **Backing:** 2⅞ yards

- **Batting:** 50″ × 50″ piece

You can include leftover scraps from Fabrics B and C if you wish.

cutting

All measurements include ¼″ seam allowances.

Cut strips on the crosswise grain of the fabric (selvage to selvage), unless otherwise noted.

Appliqué patterns for the swag, leaf, small flower, small flower center, star, star center, tulip, and tulip center appear on page 23. The pattern for the star diamond appears on page 22.

note

The star diamond pattern is marked with the letters a and b to help you orient the diamonds correctly as you construct the block. Transfer these markings to both the template and the seam allowance of the fabric pieces as you cut them.

- **From the *lengthwise grain* of the very light tone-on-tone cream print (Fabric A)**

  Cut 4 strips 8″ × 38½″.

- **From the remaining very light tone-on-tone cream print (Fabric A)**

  Cut 1 square 5¼″ × 5¼″; then cut the square in half twice diagonally to make 4 quarter-square triangles.

  Cut 4 squares 3½″ × 3½″.

  Cut 3 strips 10½″ × the fabric width; crosscut into 2 squares 10½″ × 10½″ and 2 strips 10½″ × 30½″.

- From the light-medium beige print (Fabric B)

  Cut 4 regular and 4 reverse star diamonds.

  Cut 4 small star center appliqués.

- From the light-medium beige and gray print (Fabric C)

  Cut 8 swag appliqués.

  Cut 4 small star appliqués.

  Cut 5 strips 1″ × the fabric width.

- From the medium beige and gray print (Fabric D)

  Cut 1½″-wide bias strips (page 48) to total approximately 400″.

- From the assorted light, light-medium, medium, and medium-dark neutral prints

  Cut a *total* of 20 regular and 16 reverse leaf appliqués.

  Cut a *total* of 8 small flower appliqués.

  Cut a *total* of 8 small flower center appliqués.

  Cut a *total* of 16 tulip center appliqués.

  Cut a *total* of 16 tulip appliqués.

- From the very light cream solid (Fabric E)

  Cut 5 strips 2⅛″ × the fabric width.

making the LeMoyne Star block

The ^ symbol in the following diagrams indicates which edges or points to align. The numbers indicate the sewing order, the broken arrows indicate the sewing direction, and the solid arrows indicate the pressing direction.

1. Mark a dot ¼″ in from the 90° corner on the wrong side of each Fabric A quarter-square triangle as shown. Mark a dot in one corner on the wrong side of each Fabric A square as shown. The dots will tell you where to stop or resume sewing (both with a backstitch) as you inset these background pieces into the block.

Wrong side of fabric   Wrong side of fabric

2. Sew 1 regular and 1 reverse Fabric B star diamond and a Fabric A quarter-square triangle together in the sequence shown. Make sure to match the *a* sides of the diamonds with each other and match the *b* sides of the diamonds with the short sides of the triangle. Press. Make 4.

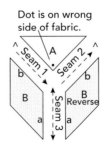

Sew seam 3 in either direction.

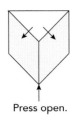

Press open.
Make 4.

3. With the dot positioned in the lower left corner to indicate where to stop and backstitch, sew a Fabric A square to each unit from Step 2. Press. Make 4.

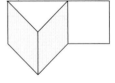

Dot is on wrong side of fabric.

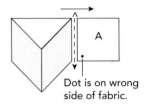

Make 4.

4. Place 2 units from Step 3 right sides together. Sew seam 1, remembering to backstitch at the dot. Pin to align the center seams exactly and sew seam 2, backstitching at the dot. Press. Make 2.

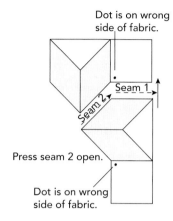

Dot is on wrong side of fabric.

Seam 1

Seam 2

Press seam 2 open.

Dot is on wrong side of fabric.

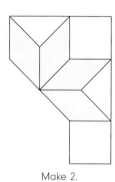

Make 2.

5. Place the units from Step 4 right sides together. Sew seams 1 and 2, remembering to backstitch at the dots. Pin to align the center seams exactly and sew seam 3, backstitching at both dots. Press.

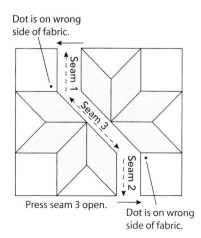

Dot is on wrong side of fabric.

Seam 1

Seam 3

Seam 2

Press seam 3 open.

Dot is on wrong side of fabric.

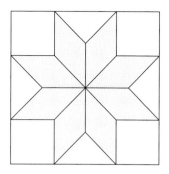

assembling and appliquéing the medallion center

Use your preferred methods for preparing and stitching the appliqués after assembling the top.

1. Sew a $10\frac{1}{2}''$ Fabric A square to the top and bottom of the LeMoyne Star block. Press. Sew a $10\frac{1}{2}'' \times 30\frac{1}{2}''$ Fabric A strip to each remaining side. Press.

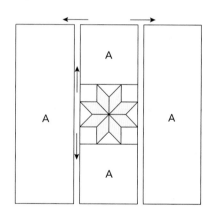

A

A

A

A

2. Referring to the photo on page 18, use your preferred method to prepare and appliqué 8 swags around the LeMoyne Star block. The swags will overlap each other, use the star points as a guide for placing them.

3. Referring to Making Bias Strips (page 49), use the $1\frac{1}{2}''$-wide Fabric D bias strips to prepare approximately 400″ of bias vine.

4. Referring again to the photo on page 18, prepare and appliqué 8 regular and 8 reverse leaves, 8 short lengths of vine from Step 3, 8 small flowers, 8 flower centers, 4 stars, and 4 star centers to the unit from Step 2.

5. Refer to Partial-Seam Borders (page 49). Beginning with the right edge and working counterclockwise, sew an $8'' \times 38\frac{1}{2}''$ Fabric A border strip to the right edge, the top edge, the left edge, and the bottom edge of the quilt. Press the seams toward the border.

6. Referring again to the photo on page 18, prepare and appliqué 12 regular and 8 reversed leaves, 16 short lengths of vine from Step 3 for stems, the remaining vine, 16 tulip centers, and 16 tulips to the quilt.

finishing

Refer to General Instructions (page 48).

1. Layer and baste your quilt.

2. Quilt as desired. Paula echo quilted around each appliqué, and she echo quilted inside the LeMoyne Star with lines spaced approximately $\frac{1}{2}''$ apart. She quilted the background of the entire quilt with a 1″ diagonal grid, breaking in only to add a feathered wreath between (and overlapping) the swag and circular vine, and a lush feather-and-cable motif over the border vine.

3. Sew the 1″-wide Fabric C strips together end-to-end with diagonal seams. Press the seams open. Fold the strip wrong sides together and press to create a long piping strip.

4. Trim the batting and backing even with the raw edge of the quilt top. Measure the quilt through the center from top to bottom and from side to side. Cut 2 strips to each measurement from the long piping strip. With right sides together and raw edges aligned, use a machine basting stitch and a scant ¼″ seam to sew the piping strips to the sides, top, and bottom of the quilt.

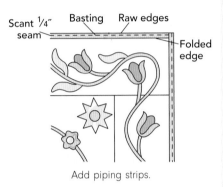

Add piping strips.

5. Sew the 2⅛″-wide Fabric E strips together end-to-end with diagonal seams and use the long strip to bind the edges.

Diamond pattern includes ¼″ seam allowance.

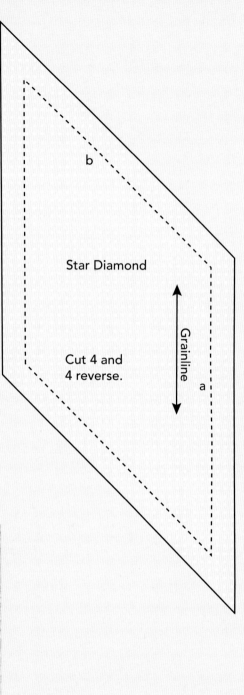

Star Diamond

Cut 4 and 4 reverse.

Grainline

Appliqué patterns do not include seam allowances.

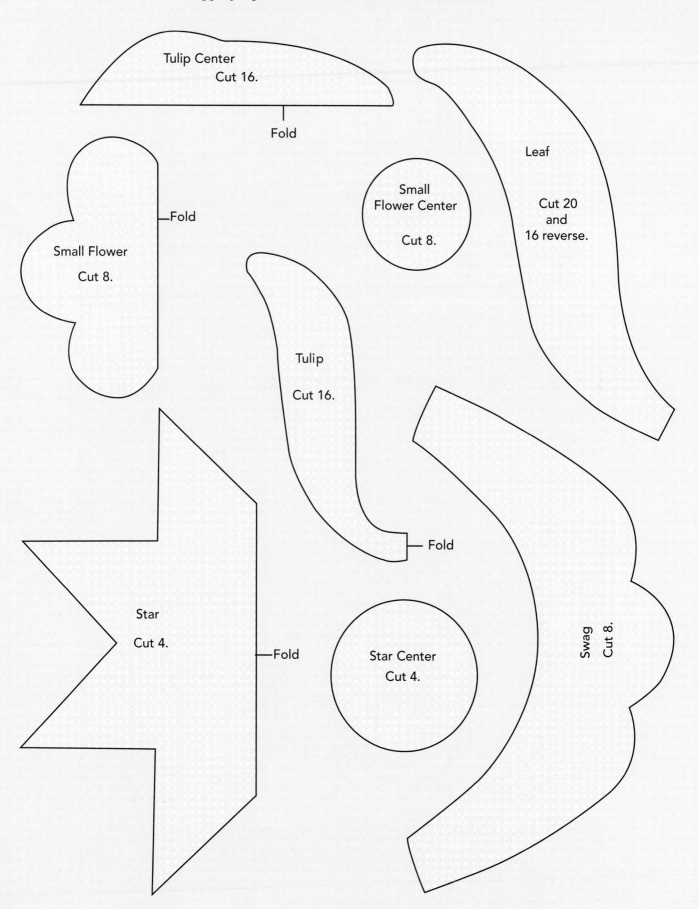

Tulip Center
Cut 16.

Fold

Small Flower
Cut 8.

Fold

Small
Flower Center

Cut 8.

Leaf

Cut 20
and
16 reverse.

Tulip

Cut 16.

Fold

Star

Cut 4.

Fold

Star Center
Cut 4.

Swag
Cut 8.

crème brulée

FINISHED QUILT SIZE $50\frac{1}{8}'' \times 62\frac{7}{8}''$ FINISHED BLOCK SIZE $8'' \times 8''$

NUMBER OF BLOCKS 18   SKILL LEVEL Confident beginner

Pieced, hand appliquéd, and machine quilted by Mary Kay Davis, 2006

met Mary Kay after she won a P&B Textiles fabric challenge. Her style is diverse, and she is *incredibly* prolific. I was thrilled that she was willing to join our adventure in making neutral quilts.

The classic Dresden Plate pattern lends itself beautifully to a neutral palette. In fact, Mary Kay explains, "I chose the Dresden Plate because I couldn't use 'color' for a quilt for this book. If you ask Alex, she may remember that she wasn't sure I'd be able to *do* a neutral quilt after seeing some of my brighter creations. I wanted to select a pattern that would let me use a multitude of fabrics in a number of different values. I tossed in everything from florals and checks to elephant and horseshoe prints. The prints and values became my colors. I'm very happy with the way the striped sashing separates the plates and seems to highlight each one.

"As for naming the quilt, I must have been starving at the time. Every name I came up with involved food (or drink): Chocolate Roses, Café au Lait, Crème de Cacao, Mocha Moonpies. Crème Brulee won out in the end. (At least these desserts are calorie-free!)"

materials

Fabric amounts are based on a 42" fabric width.

- **Assorted light and medium neutral prints:** 2⅛ yards *total* for block backgrounds and side and corner setting triangles (**Fabric A**)

- **Assorted light, medium, and medium-dark neutral prints:** 1¾ yards *total* OR 7 fat quarters for Dresden Plate petals and centers (**Fabric B**)

- **Light-medium neutral stripe:** 1⅜ yards for sashing and bias binding (**Fabric C**)

- **Medium-dark neutral print:** ⅜ yard for sashing corner squares and inner border (**Fabric D**)

- **Light neutral floral print:** 1⅔ yards for outer border (**Fabric E**)

- **Backing:** 3⅛ yards of fabric (horizontal seam); 3⅞ yards (vertical seam)

- **Batting:** 55" × 67" piece

cutting

All measurements include ¼" seam allowances.

Cut strips on the crosswise grain of the fabric (selvage to selvage), unless otherwise noted.

Patterns for the Dresden Plate petal and Dresden Plate center appliqué appear on page 28.

- **From the assorted light and medium neutral prints (Fabric A)**

  Cut a *total* of 18 squares 9½" × 9½". *

  Cut a *total* of 3 squares 14" × 14"; then cut each square in half twice diagonally to make 4 quarter-square triangles (12 total; you will have 2 triangles left over).

  Cut a *total* of 2 squares 8" × 8"; then cut each square in half once diagonally to make 2 half-square triangles (4 total).

- **From the assorted light, medium, and medium-dark neutral prints (Fabric B)**

  Cut a *total* of 216 Dresden Plate petals in matching sets of 3.

  Cut a *total* of 18 Dresden Plate centers. **

* *These squares are cut oversized and will be trimmed after the appliqué is complete.*

** *You may wish to cut these after the Dresden Plates are assembled so you can match the center to one of the petal sets in each block.*

■ **From the light-medium neutral stripe (Fabric C)**

Cut 12 strips 1½″ × the fabric width; crosscut into 48 strips 1½″ × 8½″.

Cut 2⅛″-wide bias strips (page 48) to total approximately 250″.

■ **From the medium-dark neutral print (Fabric D)**

Cut 7 strips 1½″ × the fabric width; crosscut 2 strips into 31 squares 1½″ × 1½″. Set the remaining strips aside for the inner border.

■ **From the *lengthwise grain* of the light neutral floral print (Fabric E)**

Cut 2 strips 4½″ × 50⅛″.

Cut 2 strips 4½″ × 54⅞″.

making the blocks

You will make 18 Dresden Plate blocks for this quilt. Each block uses 12 Dresden Plate petals in matching sets of 3 and an appliquéd center that matches one of the petal sets. Instructions are for 1 block.

1. With right sides together, fold a Fabric B Dresden Plate petal in half lengthwise. Finger-press. Fold 12 in 4 matching sets of 3. With a ¼″ seam, stitch across the top of each folded petal.

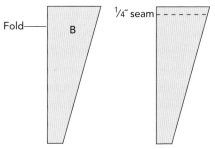

Fold 12 in 4 matching sets of 3.
Stitch.

2. Turn the petal right side out to form a point at the top. Finger-press the seam open. Make 12.

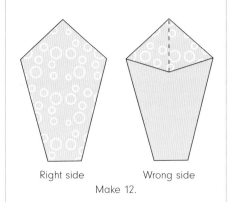

Right side   Wrong side
Make 12.

3. With right sides together, sew 2 scrappy units from Step 2 together along their long edges. Press the seams open. Make 2 sets of 3 matching pairs.

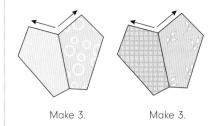

Make 3.   Make 3.

4. Lay out the pairs from Step 3 to make a Dresden Plate, alternating the pairs. Sew 3 pairs together along the long edges to make each half of the Dresden Plate.

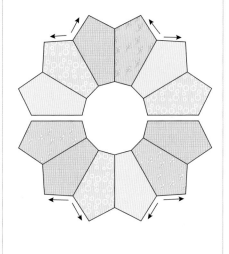

5. Sew the units from Step 4 together to complete the Dresden Plate. Press.

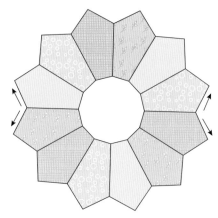

6. Repeat Steps 1–5 to make a total of 18 Dresden Plates.

appliquéing the blocks

Use your preferred methods for preparing and stitching the appliqués.

1. Fold each 9½″ Fabric A square in half vertically, horizontally, and then diagonally in both directions. Finger-press. Use the creases to place a pieced Dresden Plate and a Dresden Plate center that matches one of the petal fabrics in the center of each square, taking care to orient the Dresden Plate as shown. Pin or baste.

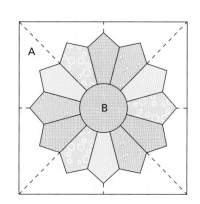

2. Use your preferred method to appliqué the Dresden Plates and centers to the blocks. Make 18. Trim the blocks to 8½″ × 8½″.

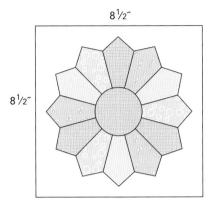

8½″

8½″

Make 18.

quilt assembly

1. Sew a Dresden Plate block between two 1½″ × 8½″ Fabric C strips. Press. Make 2.

Make 2.

2. Arrange and sew 3 Dresden Plate blocks and four 1½″ × 8½″ Fabric C strips, alternating them as shown. Press. Make 2.

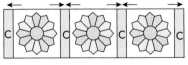

Make 2.

3. Arrange and sew 5 Dresden Plate blocks and six 1½″ × 8½″ Fabric C strips, alternating them as shown. Press. Make 2.

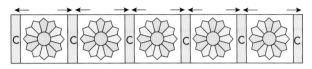

Make 2.

4. Sew a 1½″ × 8½″ Fabric C strip between two 1½″ Fabric D squares as shown. Press. Make 2. Sew 1 of these units to each unit from Step 1. Press. Make 2.

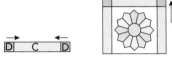

D   C   D

Make 2.   Make 2.

5. Arrange and sew three 1½″ × 8½″ Fabric C strips and four 1½″ Fabric D squares, alternating them as shown. Press. Make 2. Sew 1 of these units to each unit from Step 2. Press. Make 2.

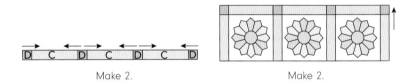

D   C   D   C   D   C   D

Make 2.   Make 2.

6. Arrange and sew five 1½″ × 8½″ Fabric C strips and six 1½″ Fabric D squares, alternating them as shown. Press. Make 2. Sew 1 unit to each unit from Step 3. Press. Make 2.

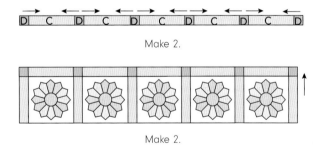

D   C   D   C   D   C   D   C   D   C   D

Make 2.

Make 2.

7. Arrange and sew six 1½″ × 8½″ Fabric C strips and seven 1½″ Fabric D squares, alternating them as shown. Press.

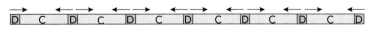

D   C   D   C   D   C   D   C   D   C   D   C   D

Make 1.

8. Arrange the units from Steps 4–7 and the assorted Fabric A side (quarter-square) and corner (half-square) setting triangles in diagonal rows as shown in the assembly diagram.

9. Sew the side setting triangles to each row to complete the row. Press. Sew the rows together. Press. Add the corner setting triangles. Press.

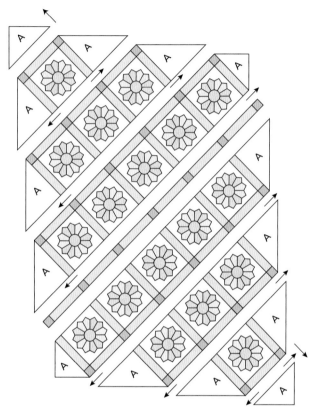

Assembly diagram

adding the borders

1. Sew the remaining 1½"-wide Fabric D strips together end-to-end. Press. From this strip, cut 2 inner-border strips 1½" × 40⅛" and 2 inner-border strips 1½" × 54⅞".

2. Sew the 1½" × 40⅛" Fabric D strips to the top and bottom of the quilt. Press the seams toward the borders. Sew the 1½" × 54⅞" Fabric D strips to the sides of the quilt. Press the seams toward the borders.

3. Sew the 4½" × 54⅞" Fabric E strips to the sides of the quilt and sew the 4½" × 50⅛" Fabric E strips to the top and bottom. Press the seams toward the newly added borders.

finishing

Refer to General Instructions (page 48).

1. Layer and baste your quilt.

2. Quilt as desired. Mary Kay anchored the key seams in her quilt (for example, around each block, between the borders, and so on) by quilting in-the-ditch. She echo quilted around every other petal in each Dresden Plate; this allowed her to quilt the Dresden Plate with a single continuous line of stitching. The setting triangles were crosshatched in a 1" diagonal grid, and a simple but effective vine-and-leaf pattern completed the outer border.

3. Sew the assorted 2⅛"-wide Fabric C bias strips together end-to-end with diagonal seams and use the long strip to bind the edges.

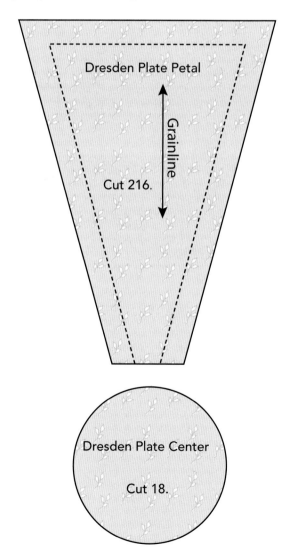

Dresden Plate Petal

Grainline

Cut 216.

Dresden Plate Center

Cut 18.

Petal pattern includes ¼" seam allowance. Center appliqué pattern does not include seam allowance.

cinnamon toast

FINISHED QUILT SIZE $42\frac{1}{2}'' \times 56\frac{1}{2}''$ FINISHED BLOCK SIZE $7'' \times 7''$

NUMBER OF BLOCKS 48   SKILL LEVEL Confident beginner

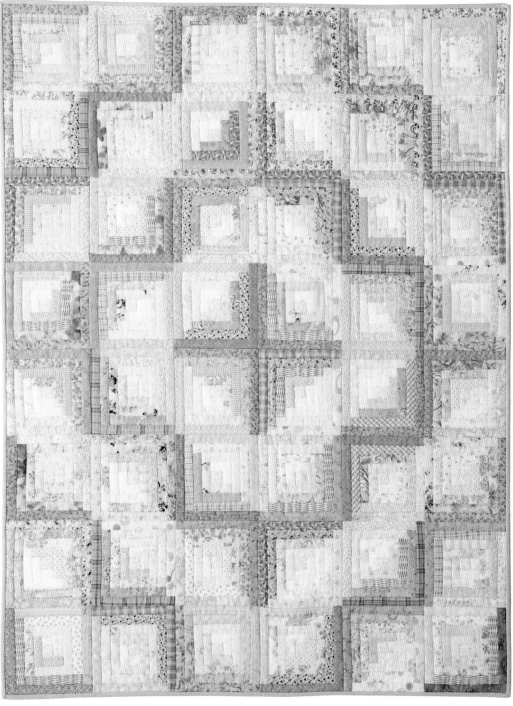

Pieced and machine quilted by Pam Vieira, 2006

The Log Cabin block is a wonderfully versatile block. I was so happy when Pam agreed to make a Log Cabin quilt entirely in neutrals for this book, as I think of this pattern as one of her specialties. She was careful with the range of value, never venturing further than the medium range. The contrast between the light and dark sides of the block is apparent but subtle, giving the quilt a soft and sophisticated look.

Asked how she found pairing this classic block with a neutral palette, Pam explained, "The Log Cabin is simple to sew, but repetitious, so it is often overlooked by novices and more experienced quilters alike. Personally, I enjoy the Log Cabin block and its many design possibilities. Creating a Log Cabin completely in neutrals was a way to explore the subtle variations of light and dark while enjoying a chance to refocus on basic machine piecing skills. While I explored many other settings, the blocks in this quilt are set in the Barn Raising design, one of many classic Log Cabin settings."

materials

Fabric amounts are based on a 42″ fabric width, unless otherwise noted.

A fat quarter measures approximately 18″ × 22″. (Note that fat quarters will create a quilt that is not as scrappy as the quilt pictured in the photo.)

- Light-medium neutral print: ¼ yard OR 1 fat quarter for block centers (**Fabric A**)

- Assorted very light to light neutral prints: 1¾ yards *total* OR 7 fat quarters for blocks (**Fabric B**)

- Assorted medium to medium-dark neutral prints: 2 yards *total* OR 8 fat quarters for blocks (**Fabric C**)

- Medium neutral check: ⅔ yard for binding (**Fabric D**)

- Backing: 3⅝ yards of fabric

- Batting: 47″ × 61″ piece

cutting

All measurements include ¼″ seam allowances.

Cut strips on the crosswise grain of the fabric (selvage to selvage), unless otherwise noted.

If you are using fat quarters, double the number of strips cut from Fabrics A, B, and C.

- From the light-medium neutral print (Fabric A)

   Cut 2 strips 1½″ × the fabric width; crosscut into 48 squares 1½″ × 1½″.

- From the assorted very light to light neutral prints (Fabric B)

   Cut a *total* of 44 strips 1¼″ × the fabric width.

- From the assorted medium to medium-dark neutral prints (Fabric C)

   Cut a *total* of 52 strips 1¼″ × the fabric width.

- From the medium neutral check (Fabric D)

   Cut 2⅛″-wide bias strips (page 48) to total approximately 217″.

making the blocks

1. Sew a 1¼″-wide Fabric B strip to each 1½″ Fabric A square. Trim the strip even with the raw edge of the square. Press. Make 48.

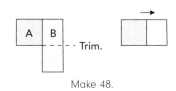

Make 48.

2. Sew a different 1¼"-wide Fabric B strip to the adjacent side of each unit from Step 1. Trim the strip even with the raw edge of the unit. Press. Make 48.

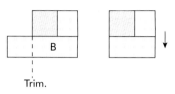

Make 48.

3. Repeat Steps 1 and 2 to sew assorted 1¼"-wide Fabric C strips to the remaining 2 sides of each unit from Step 2. Make 48.

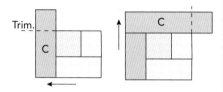

Make 48.

4. Repeat Steps 1–3 to sew two 1¼"-wide Fabric B and two 1¼"-wide Fabric C strips to each unit from Step 3. Make 48.

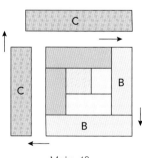

Make 48.

5. Repeat Steps 1–3 to sew two 1¼"-wide Fabric B and two 1¼"-wide Fabric C strips to each unit from Step 4. Make 48.

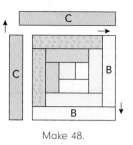

Make 48.

6. Repeat Steps 1–3 to sew two 1¼"-wide Fabric B and two 1¼"-wide Fabric C strips to each unit from Step 5 as shown. Make 48.

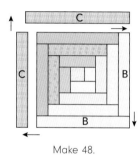

Make 48.

quilt assembly

Arrange the blocks in 8 horizontal rows of 6 blocks each, orienting the blocks as shown in the assembly diagram. Sew the blocks together into rows. Press the seams in opposite directions from row to row. Sew the rows together. Press.

Assembly diagram

finishing

Refer to General Instructions (page 48).

1. Layer and baste your quilt.

2. Quilt as desired. Pam quilted each block in-the-ditch in concentric squares to give the quilt its wonderful texture.

3. Sew the 2⅛"-wide Fabric D bias strips together end-to-end with diagonal seams and use the long strip to bind the edges.

suzanne

FINISHED QUILT SIZE $48\frac{1}{2}'' \times 64\frac{1}{2}''$ FINISHED BLOCK SIZE $16'' \times 16''$

NUMBER OF BLOCKS 6   SKILL LEVEL Confident beginner

Pieced by Dee Christopher and machine quilted by Faye Collinsworth, 2006

It was a joy to watch this quilt being "born." Rather than heading to the books for pattern ideas, Dee went to work with pencil and paper and came up with this great design. The strong diagonal movement in the block gives the quilt incredible graphic appeal, but I guess I'll let Dee tell the story: "I spent a lot of time looking at different quilt blocks to see what I thought would make an interesting quilt. Then I began playing on graph paper until I ended up with the pattern I chose. I liked the way it created a secondary design when the blocks were sewn together.

"Coming up with the border was the most difficult part for me; I finally got the expert advice I needed. I discovered I like working with beige!"

materials

Fabric amounts are based on a 42" fabric width.

A fat quarter measures approximately 18" × 22".

Cut all strips on the crosswise grain of the fabric (selvage to selvage), unless otherwise noted.

- **Assorted white-on-white and light neutral prints:** 1¼ yards *total* OR 5 fat quarters for blocks and border (**Fabric A**)

- **Assorted medium and dark neutral prints:** 1¾ yards *total* OR 7 fat quarters for blocks and border (**Fabric B**)

- **White-on-white print:** 1½ yards for border (**Fabric C**)

- **Medium neutral print:** ½ yard for binding (**Fabric D**)

- **Backing:** 3⅛ yards of fabric (horizontal seam); 4 yards (vertical seam)

- **Batting:** 53" × 69" piece

cutting

All measurements include ¼" seam allowances.

- **From the assorted white-on-white and light neutral prints (Fabric A)**

  Cut a *total* of 48 rectangles 2½" × 4½".

  Cut a *total* of 16 squares 4⅞" × 4⅞"; then cut each square in half once diagonally to make 2 half-square triangles (32 total).

  Cut a *total* of 24 squares 2⅞" × 2⅞"; then cut each square in half once diagonally to make 2 half-square triangles (48 total).

  Cut a *total* of 24 squares 2½" × 2½".

  Cut a *total* of 8 squares 4½" × 4½".

- **From the assorted medium and dark neutral prints (Fabric B)**

  Cut a *total* of 128 rectangles 2½" × 4½".

  Cut a *total* of 16 squares 4⅞" × 4⅞"; then cut each square in half once diagonally to make 2 half-square triangles (32 total).

  Cut a *total* of 24 squares 2⅞" × 2⅞"; then cut each square in half once diagonally to make 2 half-square triangles (48 total).

  Cut a *total* of 24 squares. 2½" × 2½".

- **From the *lengthwise grain* of the white-on-white print (Fabric C)**

  Cut 2 strips 4½" × 48½".

  Cut 2 strips 4½" × 32½".

- **From the medium neutral print (Fabric D)**

  Cut 6 strips 2⅛" × the fabric width.

making the blocks

1. Arrange and sew 2 assorted 2½" × 4½" Fabric A rectangles and 2 assorted 2½" × 4½" Fabric B rectangles together, alternating them as shown. Press. Make 24.

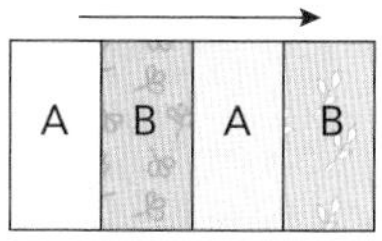

Make 24.

2. Sew a large Fabric A half-square triangle and a large Fabric B half-square triangle together along the long edges. Press. Make 32 scrappy half-square triangle units. Set 8 aside for the border.

Make 32.

3. Repeat Step 2 using the small Fabric A and Fabric B half-square triangles. Make 48.

Make 48.

4. Arrange and sew 2 units from Step 3, a 2½″ Fabric A square, and a 2½″ Fabric B square together, orienting the units and squares as shown. Press. Make 12 of each.

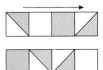

Make 12 of each.

5. Arrange and sew 2 of each unit from Step 4 together, orienting the units as shown. Press. Make 6.

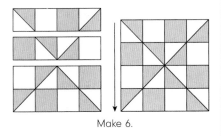

Make 6.

6. Sew a unit from Step 5 between 2 units from Step 1, orienting the units from Step 1 as shown. Press. Make 6.

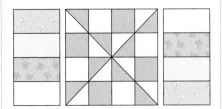

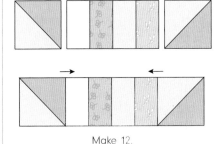

Make 6.

7. Sew a remaining unit from Step 1 between 2 units from Step 2, orienting the units as shown. Press. Make 12.

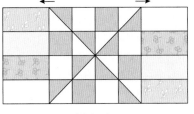

Make 12.

8. Sew a unit from Step 6 between 2 units from Step 7, orienting the units as shown. Press. Make 6.

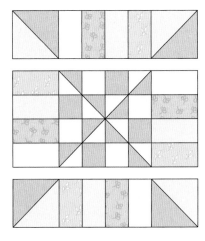

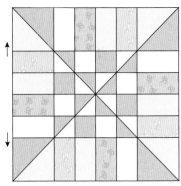

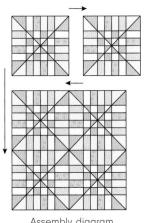

Make 6.

quilt assembly

Arrange the blocks in 3 horizontal rows of 2 blocks each as shown in the assembly diagram. Sew the blocks together into rows. Press the seams in opposite directions from row to row. Sew the rows together. Press.

Assembly diagram

making and adding borders

1. Sew 24 assorted 2½″ × 4½″ Fabric B rectangles together to make a border unit. Press. Make 2.

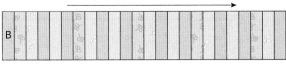

Make 2.

2. Sew each border unit from Step 1 to a 4½″ × 48½″ Fabric C strip along the long edges. Press the seams toward the Fabric C strips. Make 2.

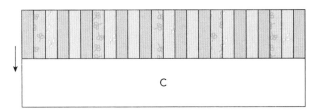

Make 2.

3. Referring to the photo on page 32, sew the border units to the sides of the quilt. Press the seams toward the border units.

4. Repeat Step 1 using 16 assorted 2½″ × 4½″ Fabric B rectangles. Make 2. Sew each border unit to a 4½″ × 32½″ Fabric C strip along the long edges. Press.

5. Arrange and sew 2 of the remaining large half-square triangle units and 2 assorted 4½″ Fabric A squares together as shown. Press. Make 4.

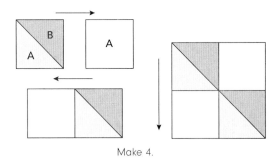

Make 4.

6. Sew a unit from Step 5 to each end of a border unit from Step 4. Press. Make 2. Sew a border unit to the top and bottom of the quilt. Press.

Make 2.

finishing

Refer to General Instructions (page 48).

1. Layer and baste your quilt.

2. Quilt as desired. Faye machine quilted a continuous interlocking square pattern over the blocks. The borders are quilted in 2 complementary heart-and-ribbon motifs.

3. Sew the assorted 2⅛″-wide Fabric D strips together end-to-end with diagonal seams and use the long strip to bind the edges.

daisy chain

FINISHED QUILT SIZE 53″ × 60″   FINISHED BLOCK SIZE $3\frac{1}{2}″ × 3\frac{1}{2}″$

NUMBER OF PIECED BLOCKS 158   NUMBER OF APPLIQUÉD BLOCKS 97   SKILL LEVEL Confident beginner

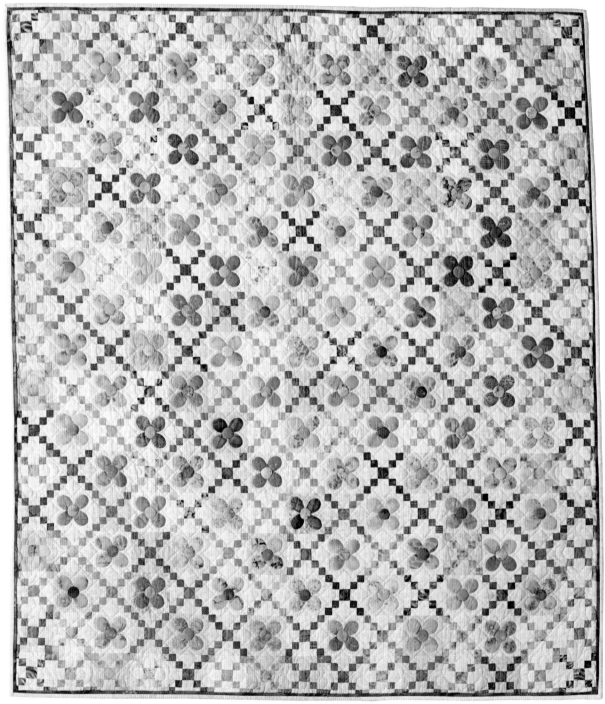

Pieced, appliquéd, and machine quilted by Alex Anderson, 2005

ometimes quilts are just *meant* to happen! A while back, I ran across some throw pillows featuring a darling little daisy shape. As I quickly sketched the basic design, I knew it would make a terrific quilt. Shortly afterward, while browsing at Back Porch Fabrics, a fabulous quilt shop in Pacific Grove, California, I discovered (and naturally purchased!) some yummy Japanese-style prints in soft, inviting neutrals. When I looked at my daisy design with those gorgeous fabrics in hand, *Daisy Chain* was a slam dunk.

I used a wide variety of neutrals in this quilt, ranging from creamy white to café au lait. I pushed the palette by including a few gray prints as well, some with bluish undertones.

materials

Fabric amounts are based on a 42″ fabric width.

A fat quarter measures approximately 18″ × 22″.

- **Assorted very light neutral prints:** 4⅝ yards *total* OR 19 fat quarters for blocks and binding **(Fabric A)**
- **Assorted light and medium neutral prints:** 3¾ yards *total* OR 15 fat quarters for blocks and appliqués **(Fabric B)**
- **Medium neutral print:** ¼ yard for flat piping **(Fabric C)**
- **Backing:** 3⅜ yards of fabric (horizontal seam); 3¾ yards (vertical seam)
- **Batting:** 57″ × 64″ piece

cutting

All measurements include ¼″ seam allowances.

Cut strips on the crosswise grain of the fabric (selvage to selvage).

Appliqué patterns for the daisy center and daisy petal appear on page 39.

- **From the assorted very light neutral prints (Fabric A)**

    Cut a *total* of 158 strips 1⅛″ × 12″.*

    Cut a *total* of 632 rectangles 1½″ × 1¾″ in matching sets of 4.*

    Cut a *total* of 97 squares 4″ × 4″.

    Cut assorted 2⅛″-wide strips to total approximately 247″.

- **From the assorted light to medium neutral prints (Fabric B)**

    Cut a *total* of 158 strips 1⅛″ × 12″.**

    Cut a *total* of 158 squares 1½″ × 1½″.**

    Cut a *total* of 97 daisy centers.

    Cut a *total* of 388 daisy petals in matching sets of 4.

- **From the medium neutral print (Fabric C)**

    Cut 6 strips 1″ × the fabric width.

    * Cut these in matching sets of one 12″-long strip and four 1½″ × 1¾″ rectangles.

    ** Cut these in matching sets of one 12″-long strip and one 1½″ square.

making the pieced blocks

1. Sew one 1⅛″ × 12″ Fabric A strip and one 1⅛″ × 12″ Fabric B strip together to make a strip set. Press. Cut the strip set into eight 1⅛″ segments.

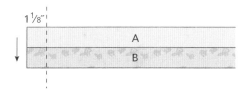

Cut 8 segments.

2. Sew 2 units from Step 1 together to make a four-patch unit. Press. Make 4.

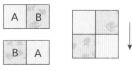

Make 4.

3. Arrange the 4 units from Step 2, four $1\frac{1}{2}'' \times 1\frac{3}{4}''$ Fabric A rectangles, and one $1\frac{1}{2}''$ Fabric B square as shown. Sew the units, rectangles, and square together into rows. Press. Sew the rows together. Press.

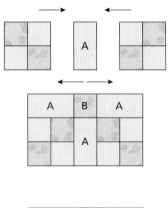

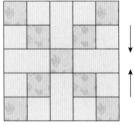

4. Repeat Steps 1–3 to make a total of 158 pieced blocks.

making the appliquéd blocks

1. Fold each 4″ Fabric A square in half vertically, horizontally, and then diagonally in both directions. Finger-press. Use the creases to place 4 matching daisy petals and a daisy center in a different fabric in the center of each square. Pin or baste.

2. Use your preferred method to appliqué the petals and centers to the blocks. Make 97.

Make 97.

quilt assembly

Arrange the pieced blocks and the appliquéd blocks in 17 horizontal rows of 15 blocks each, placing them as shown in the assembly diagram. Sew the blocks together into rows. Press the seams in opposite directions from row to row. Sew the rows together. Press.

Assembly diagram

finishing

Refer to General Instructions (pages 48).

1. Layer and baste your quilt.

2. Quilt as desired. I echo quilted around each daisy and quilted diagonally in both directions through the blocks, including the appliqué backgrounds, in the center of the quilt. For the outer edges, I chose a flower-like double-feather motif to carry on the daisy theme.

3. Sew the 1″-wide Fabric C strips together end-to-end with diagonal seams. Press the seams open. Fold the strip wrong sides together and press to create a long piping strip.

4. Trim the batting and backing even with the raw edge of the quilt top. Measure the quilt through the center from top to bottom and from side to side. Cut 2 strips to each measurement from the long piping strip. With right sides together and raw edges aligned, use a machine basting stitch and a scant ¼″ seam to sew the piping strips to the sides, top, and bottom of the quilt.

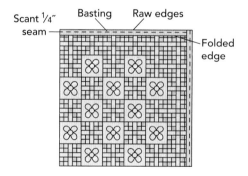

5. Sew the assorted 2⅛″-wide Fabric A strips together end-to-end with diagonal seams and use the long strip to bind the edges.

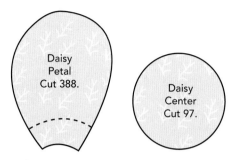

Daisy Petal Cut 388.

Daisy Center Cut 97.

Patterns do not include seam allowances.

Detail of flower/feather motif

stars and pinwheels

FINISHED QUILT SIZE $52\frac{1}{2}'' \times 52\frac{1}{2}''$ FINISHED BLOCK SIZE $4'' \times 4''$

NUMBER OF SAWTOOTH STAR BLOCKS 53   NUMBER OF PINWHEEL BLOCKS 37   SKILL LEVEL Confident beginner

Pieced and hand quilted by Alex Anderson, 1987

I made this quilt in 1987, shortly after completing my very first neutral quilt—which shows just how timeless a neutral palette can be. Because the Sawtooth Star block has no strong diagonal element, I decided to mix it up with Pinwheels and half-square-triangle units to give the overall design a sense of movement.

When my friend Diana McClun saw the blocks on my design wall, she asked whether I could finish the quilt in a month for the book she was co-authoring with Laura Nownes, *Quilts! Quilts!! Quilts!!!* (see Recommended Reading on (page 54). Of course, I agreed. In a month's time, the quilt was completely pieced, hand quilted, and ready to make its debut.

Putting this quilt together is like doing a big jigsaw puzzle—you'll assemble it in sections instead of traditional rows.

materials

Fabric amounts are based on a 42" fabric width.

A fat quarter measures approximately 18" × 22".

- **Assorted very light, light, light-medium, and medium neutral prints:** 5 yards *total* OR 20 fat quarters for blocks, filler strips, inner border, pieced outer border, and corners **(Fabric A)**

- **Medium neutral polka dot and striped print:** ¾ yard for binding **(Fabric B)**

- **Backing:** 3¼ yards of fabric

- **Batting:** 57" × 57" piece

cutting

All measurements include ¼" seam allowances.

Cut strips on the crosswise grain of the fabric (selvage to selvage), unless otherwise noted.

- **From the assorted very light, light, light-medium, and medium neutral prints (Fabric A)**

  Cut a *total* of 424 squares 1½" × 1½" in matching sets of 8 **(Fabric A1).****

  Cut a *total* of 53 squares 2½" × 2½" **(Fabric A1).****

  Cut a *total* of 212 rectangles 1½" × 2½" in matching sets of 4 **(Fabric A2).***

  Cut a *total* of 212 squares 1½" × 1½" in matching sets of 4 **(Fabric A2).***

  Cut a *total* of 421 squares 2⅞" × 2⅞" in matching sets of 2 (you will have one "odd" square); then cut each square in half once diagonally to make 2 half-square triangles (842 total).

  Cut 1½"-wide strips to total approximately 200".

- **From the medium neutral polka dot and striped print (Fabric B)**

  Cut 2⅛"-wide bias strips (page 48) to total approximately 225".

  * Cut these in matching sets of four 1½" × 2½" rectangles and four 1½" squares.

  ** Cut these in matching sets of eight 1½" squares and one 2½" square.

making the sawtooth star blocks

You will make 53 Sawtooth Star blocks for this quilt. Each block is made from 2 different Fabric A prints, referred to here as Fabric A1 and Fabric A2. Instructions are for one block.

1. Draw a line diagonally, from corner to corner, on the wrong side of each of 8 matching 1½" Fabric A1 squares.

2. Place a marked square right sides together with a contrasting 1½" × 2½" Fabric A2 rectangle as shown. Stitch directly on the drawn line and trim, leaving a ¼" seam allowance. Press. Make 4 matching units.

Make 4.

3. Repeat Step 2 to sew a remaining marked Fabric A1 square to the opposite side of each unit from Step 2. Press. Make 4.

Make 4.

4. Sew a unit from Step 3 between 2 matching 1½″ Fabric A2 squares. Press. Make 2.

Make 2.

5. Sew a matching 2½″ Fabric A1 square between the remaining 2 units from Step 3, orienting them as shown. Press.

   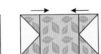
Make 2.

6. Sew the units from Step 4 to the top and bottom of the unit from Step 5 orienting them as shown. Press.

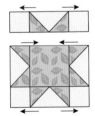 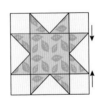
Make 25.

7. Repeat Steps 1–6 to make a total of 53 blocks. Make 25 blocks with the medium fabric as the star as shown above. Make 28 blocks with the medium fabric as the background as shown below.

Make 28.

making the pinwheel blocks

1. Sew 2 contrasting Fabric A half-square triangles together along the long edges as shown. Press. Make 421 in matching sets of 4. (You will have one "odd" half-square triangle unit.)

Make 421.

2. Arrange 4 matching half-square-triangle units from Step 1 as shown. Sew the units together into rows. Press. Sew the rows together. Press. Make 37. Set the remaining units aside for the filler strips, pieced outer border, and corner squares.

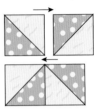
Make 37.

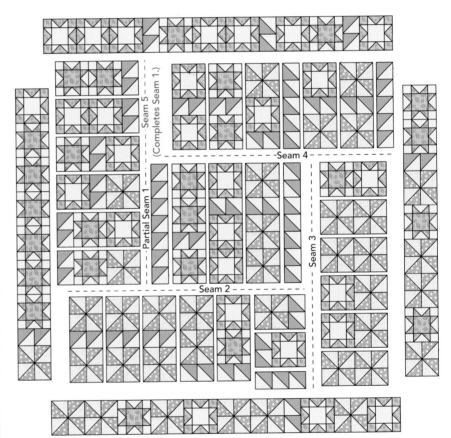
Assembly diagram

quilt assembly

1. This quilt is assembled in sections. Arrange the blocks and half-square-triangle units as shown in the assembly diagram. Within each section, sew the blocks and half-square triangles together in rows. Whenever possible, press the seams in opposite directions from row to row.

2. Sew the sections together in the order shown. Sew a partial seam where indicated. Complete the partial seam when all sections are joined. Press.

adding the borders

1. Refer to Mitered Borders (page 50). Sew the assorted $1\frac{1}{2}$"-wide Fabric A strips together end-to-end. Press. From this strip, cut 4 inner-border strips $1\frac{1}{2}$" × $48\frac{1}{2}$". Sew the borders to the sides, top, and bottom of the quilt, mitering the corners. Press the seams toward the border.

2. Sew 22 leftover half-square-triangle units together as shown to make a pieced border row. Make 4 rows, pressing the seams in one direction for 2 rows (row 1) and in the opposite direction for the remaining 2 rows (row 2).

Make 2 of each.

3. Sew a row 1 and a row 2 together to make a border unit. Press. Make 2.

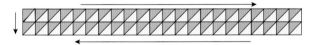

Make 2.

4. Referring to the photo on page 40, sew the border units from Step 3 to the sides of the quilt, taking care to orient the rows as shown. Press the seams toward the inner border.

5. Repeat Step 3 and Step 4 to make 2 additional border units. Notice that the triangles are oriented in the opposite direction from those in the previous borders.

Make 2.

6. Arrange 4 remaining half-square-triangle units as shown. Sew the units together into rows. Press. Sew the rows together to make a corner unit. Press. Make 4.

Make 4.

7. Referring to the photo on page 40, sew a corner unit from Step 6 to each end of a border unit from Step 5. Press the seams toward the corner units. Make 2 and sew them to the top and bottom of the quilt. Press.

finishing

Refer to General Instructions (page 48).

1. Layer and baste your quilt.

2. Quilt as desired. I hand quilted the center of the quilt with an allover pattern of wavy lines and covered the inner and outer borders with a sawtooth pattern that echoed the half-square triangle units.

3. Sew the $2\frac{1}{8}$"-wide Fabric B bias strips together end-to-end with diagonal seams and use the long strip to bind the edges.

mama's spool box

FINISHED QUILT SIZE 28″ × 28″   FINISHED BLOCK SIZE 5″ × 5″

NUMBER OF SPOOL BLOCKS 9   SKILL LEVEL Confident beginner

Pieced, machine quilted, and embellished by Darra Williamson, 2006

arra's quilt would make a wonderful class for introducing neutrals. The blocks are simple to piece, the overall size is small, and the design depends on contrast in value—a key lesson in working with neutrals—to achieve a dimensional effect.

The pattern was a sentimental choice for Darra, who explains, "My mother was an expert seamstress, and made many of the clothes my sisters and I wore growing up. She was the *best*: no one would ever have guessed our clothes were homemade except for our pride in announcing 'Mom made it!' Sewing was her creative outlet, and we loved to rummage through her patterns and buttons, threads and trims while she worked at the machine. This one's for you, Mom."

materials

Fabric amounts are based on a 42" fabric width.

- Assorted very light, light, light-medium neutral prints: ¹⁄₃ yard *total* for blocks (**Fabric A**)

- Assorted light-medium and medium neutral prints: ¹⁄₄ yard *total* for blocks (**Fabric B**)

- Assorted medium and medium-dark neutral prints: ¹⁄₄ yard *total* for blocks (**Fabric C**)

- Medium neutral prints: ¹⁄₄ yard *each* of 2 slightly contrasting fabrics for inner border (**Fabric D1 and Fabric D2**)

- Light neutral subtle stripe: 1 yard for outer border (**Fabric E**)

- Medium neutral print: ¹⁄₃ yard for binding (**Fabric F**)

- Backing: 1 yard of fabric

- Batting: 32" × 32" piece

- ¹⁄₄"-wide rickrack: 3¹⁄₂ yards each of 2 contrasting colors

- Buttons: 16–20 assorted (optional)

- Embroidery floss: neutral color (optional)

cutting

All measurements include ¹⁄₄" seam allowances.

Cut strips on the crosswise grain of the fabric (selvage to selvage), unless otherwise noted.

- From the assorted very light, light, light-medium, and medium neutral prints (Fabric A)

  Cut a *total* of 18 rectangles 1¹⁄₂" × 3¹⁄₂" in matching pairs.*

  Cut a *total* of 36 squares 1¹⁄₂" × 1¹⁄₂" in matching sets of 4.*

- From the assorted light-medium and medium neutral prints (Fabric B)

  Cut a *total* of 9 squares 3¹⁄₂" × 3¹⁄₂".

- From the assorted medium and medium-dark neutral prints (Fabric C)

  Cut a *total* of 18 rectangles 1¹⁄₂" × 5¹⁄₂" in matching pairs.

- From *each* of the slightly contrasting medium and/or medium-dark neutral prints (Fabrics D1 and D2)

  Cut 2 strips 2" × 30".

- From the *lengthwise grain* of the light neutral subtle stripe (Fabric E)**

  Cut 4 strips 5¹⁄₄" × 30".

- From the medium neutral print (Fabric F)

  Cut 4 strips 2¹⁄₈" × the fabric width.

* Cut these in matching sets of two 1¹⁄₂" × 3¹⁄₂" rectangles (1 pair) and four 1¹⁄₂" squares.

** Depending upon how the stripe runs in your fabric and the look you want, you may prefer to cut these strips on the crosswise grain instead.

making the spool blocks

1. Sew a 3½″ Fabric B square between 2 matching 1½″ × 3½″ Fabric A rectangles. Press.

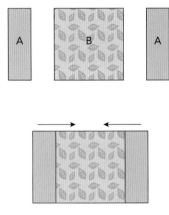

Make 1.

2. Draw a line diagonally, from corner to corner, on the wrong side of each of 4 matching 1½″ Fabric A squares. These squares should match the Fabric A rectangles in Step 1.

3. Place a marked square right sides together on each end of a 1½″ × 5½″ Fabric C rectangle as shown. Stitch directly on the drawn lines and trim, leaving a ¼″ seam allowance. Press. Make 2 matching units.

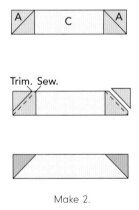

Trim. Sew.

Make 2.

4. Sew the units from Step 3 to the top and bottom of the unit from Step 1 as shown. Press.

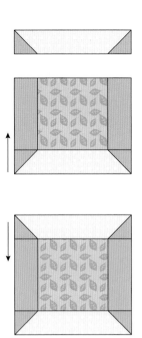

Make 1.

5. Repeat Steps 1–4 to make a total of 9 blocks.

quilt assembly

1. Arrange the blocks in 3 horizontal rows of 3 blocks each, rotating them as shown in the assembly diagram. Sew the blocks together into rows. Press the seams open. Sew the rows together. Press.

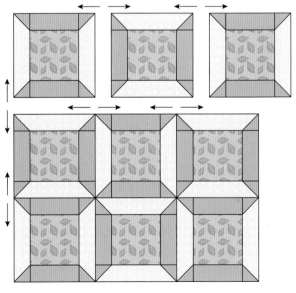

Assembly diagram

2. Sew a 2″ × 30″ Fabric D1 strip and a 5¼″ × 30″ Fabric E strip together along the long edges to make a border unit. Press the seam toward the darker fabric. Make 2. Repeat using the 2″ × 30″ Fabric D2 strips and the remaining 5¼″ × 30″ Fabric E strips.

3. Refer to Mitered Borders (page 50). Sew the Fabric D1/Fabric E border units to opposite sides of the unit from Step 1 and sew the Fabric D2/Fabric E border units to the remaining sides of the unit, mitering the corners.

finishing

Refer to General Instructions (page 48).

1. Layer and baste your quilt.

2. Quilt as desired. Darra quilted in-the-ditch around all the block elements and on each side of the inner border. She quilted each spool in a zigzag pattern that mimics thread. Rather than quilting the outer border, she used various neutral-colored threads and a narrow zigzag stitch to tack the layers.

3. Sew the 2⅛″-wide Fabric F strips together end-to-end with diagonal seams and use the long strip to bind the edges.

4. Cut each piece of rickrack into 4 equal pieces. Referring to the photo on page 44, position, pin, and topstitch each piece of rickrack to the quilt with matching colored thread. Add additional decorative stitching and attach buttons with embroidery floss as desired.

tip

If you can't find rickrack in an appropriate neutral shade, buy white and dye it with tea.

Detail of embellishment

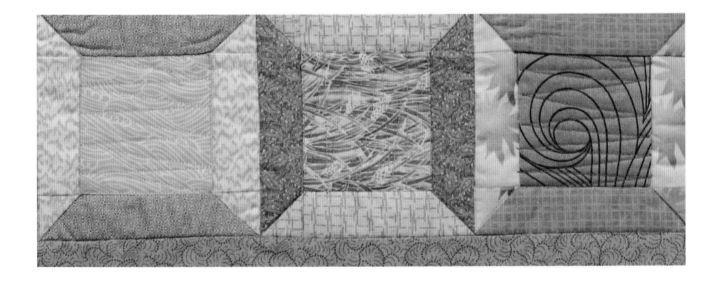

general instructions

rotary cutting

If you've never used a rotary cutter before, you might want to read *Rotary Cutting with Alex Anderson* (see Recommended Reading on page 54). Practice on some scrap fabric before starting on your project.

pinning

Some quilters pin and some quilters don't. I am a firm believer in pinning wherever there are seams and at intersections that need to line up.

I strongly recommend that you invest in a package or two of quality pins. My favorites are extra-fine (1⅜″/0.50mm) glass-head pins. They are a bit more expensive than other pins, but believe me, they are worth the investment.

piecing

Set the stitch length on your sewing machine just long enough so your seam ripper will slide nicely under the stitch. Backstitching is not necessary if the seam ends will be crossed by other seams.

pressing

I usually press seams to one side or the other, but in some cases—for example, if six or more seams are converging in one area—I press the seams open to reduce the bulk. I've included arrows on the illustrations to indicate which way to press the seams.

bias strips

cutting bias strips

1. Straighten the edge of the fabric. Place the fabric on your cutting mat, aligning the straightened edge of the fabric with a horizontal line on the mat. Position your ruler so the 45° marking is aligned with the straight edge of the fabric. Make a cut.

2. Move the ruler over and align the measurement for the strip width, 2⅛″ in this example, with the trimmed 45° fabric edge. Cut the strip. Continue cutting until you have the number of strips needed to bind your quilt.

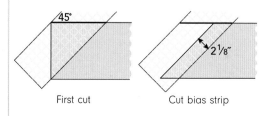

First cut   Cut bias strip

making bias strips

Use this method to make bias vines and stems for *LeMoyne Star Appliqué Medallion* (page 18).

1. Cut bias strips to the width and length listed in the project cutting instructions. If necessary, piece the strips with diagonal seams to achieve the required length. Use the method described in Binding (Step 3, page 52).

2. With wrong sides together, fold the strip in half lengthwise and press. Carefully sew a seam ¼″ from the long raw edge.

3. Insert a bias bar into the fabric tube and roll the seam to the top side of the bar as shown, trimming the seam if necessary. Press the strip (I like to use steam). As each section is pressed, move the bar down the fabric tube and press again. Take care if you are using a metal bias bar because it will get very hot.

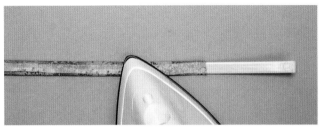

Insert bias bar and press.

borders

The quilts in this book feature four different border treatments: butted borders, borders with corner squares, partial-seam borders, and mitered borders. Because most quilters are familiar with butted borders and borders with corner squares, these are covered in the instructions and diagrams that appear with the projects that use them. Detailed instructions for partial-seam borders and mitered borders appear here.

partial-seam borders

1. Measure your quilt top from top to bottom through the center. To this measurement, add the finished width of the border. Cut the side borders to this length.

2. Measure your quilt top from side to side through the center. To this measurement, add the finished width of the border. Cut the top and bottom borders to this length.

3. Find and mark the midpoint on each side of the quilt top.

4. From one end of each side border, measure and mark the *length* of the quilt top. Find and crease the midpoint between the end of the strip and the point you've just marked. Repeat for the top and bottom borders, measuring and marking the *width* of the quilt top and creasing to find the midpoint.

5. Place a side border and the right edge of the quilt top right sides together. Match the midpoints and then match the bottom right corner of the quilt top with the marked endpoint on the border, and pin. (The border will extend beyond the bottom edge of the quilt.) Align the opposite end of the border strip with the top right corner of the quilt, and pin as needed.

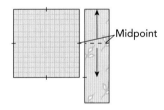

6. Stitch the border strip to the quilt top, stopping approximately 3″ from the corner of the quilt top. Press.

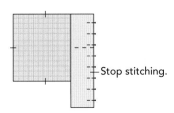

7. Place the top border and the top edge of the quilt top right sides together. Match the midpoints and then match the ends of the border with the corners of the quilt. Pin as needed.

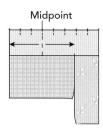

Midpoint

8. Stitch the border to the quilt. Press.

9. Repeat to add the left side border and the bottom border.

10. Complete the first border seam. If necessary, trim and square the corners of the quilt.

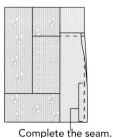

Complete the seam.

mitered borders

Mitered borders have corner seams angled at 45°, so the border corner resembles a picture frame. These borders are a little trickier than other types of borders, but the results are well worth the effort.

1. Measure your quilt top from top to bottom through the center. To this measurement, add two times the finished width of the border, plus an extra 2″–3″ for seam allowances and "insurance." Cut the side borders to this length.

2. Measure your quilt from side to side through the center. To this measurement, add two times the finished width of the border, plus an extra 2″–3″ for seam allowances and "insurance." Cut the top and bottom borders to this length.

3. Find and mark the midpoint on each side of the quilt top and the midpoint of each border strip. From the marked midpoint on each side border, measure in both directions and mark half the *length* of the quilt top. Repeat, using the *width* of the quilt top to measure and mark the top and bottom borders.

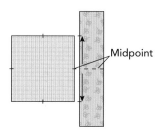

Midpoint

4. Place a side border and the quilt top right sides together. Match and pin the midpoints and then match the corners of the quilt top with the marked ends of the border strip. The border will extend beyond the edges of the quilt top. Use additional pins as needed.

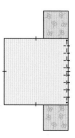

5. Stitch the border to the quilt top. Start and end the seam with a backstitch, ¼″ in from the corners of the quilt top. Press. Repeat for the other side and for the top and bottom borders.

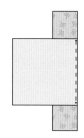

6. Place a corner of the quilt top right side up on your ironing board. Place one border strip on top of the neighboring border strip.

7. Fold the top border strip under, so that it forms a 45° angle, and press lightly. Use a ruler with a 45° marking to check that the angle is accurate and that the corner of the quilt is flat and square. Make any necessary adjustments. When you're sure everything is in place, firmly press the fold.

45°

8. From the corner, fold the quilt top on the diagonal, right sides together, aligning the long raw edges of the neighboring border strips. The crease you've pressed in the border should form a perfect extension of the diagonal fold in the quilt top. Pin to secure the folded corner of the border for stitching.

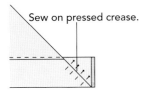

Sew on pressed crease.

9. To sew the miter, begin at the inside corner, at the point where the border seams meet. Backstitch and then stitch along the crease toward the outside corner of the border. You'll be stitching on the bias, so be careful not to stretch the fabric as you sew. Finish with another backstitch.

10. Trim the excess border fabric to leave a ¼″ seam allowance and press the seam open.

Trim.

11. Repeat Steps 6–10 to miter the remaining corners.

layering and basting

I typically cut my batting and backing 2″ larger than the quilt top on all sides. The amounts shown in the materials listing for each project include this extra "insurance."

Spread the backing wrong side up on your (nonloop) carpet or work surface. Smooth the backing and secure it with T-pins or masking tape. Center the batting on top of the backing and trim the two layers so the raw edges match. Center the quilt top right side up on the batting, smoothing carefully to remove any wrinkles.

For hand quilting, use large hand stitches to baste the three layers together in a 4″ gridded pattern. For machine quilting, secure the three layers every 3″ with rust-proof size no. 1 safety pins. Distribute the pins evenly, avoiding areas where you know you'll be stitching. For both hand and machine quilting, baste all the way to the edges of the quilt top.

quilting your neutral quilt

There are a few special considerations to keep in mind as you decide how to quilt your neutral quilt. For this reason, you'll probably want to begin thinking about potential quilting motifs and an overall quilting strategy right from the get-go.

Because both the palette and the resulting degree of contrast in these quilts tend to be more subtle than in the typical, highly colored quilt, the quilting on an all-neutral quilt *really* shows. In fact, the lower the degree of contrast in the fabrics, the more visible the quilting will be.

I consider this to be a real advantage rather than an obstacle. Consider the quilt top as a wonderful canvas for rich, dense quilting. Crosshatching, feathered wreaths, cables, lush flowering vines—all are fabulous choices for neutral quilts. The hills and valleys created by the quilting stitches cast subtle shadows and add a luxurious texture to the finished surface.

Detail of quilting from *Stars and Pinwheels* (page 40)

Detail of quilting from *Suzanne* (page 32)

Detail of quilting from *LeMoyne Star Appliqué Medallion* (page 18)

I love to hand quilt, but unfortunately I don't always have time. I usually determine how the quilt will be used and then decide how to handle the quilting. Whether you hand or machine quilt, I have three thoughts to share:

1. When it comes to quilting, more is better. Never skimp on the amount of quilting on your quilt.

2. Treat the surface as a whole. I often quilt my quilts with interesting grids that unify the design. On the other hand, I rarely quilt within $1/4''$ of the seamlines, because this accentuates what to me is the most unsightly part of the quilt—the seams.

3. Use an equal amount of quilting over the entire surface. If you quilt different areas with unequal density, your quilt not only will look odd but will also sag and not lie flat.

binding

1. Trim the batting and backing even with the raw edge of the quilt top.

2. Cut $2^{1}/8''$-wide strips from the fabric width, or the bias, as directed in the project instructions.

3. Sew the strips together end-to-end with a diagonal seam and press the seams open. Pressing this way will help prevent big lumps in the binding.

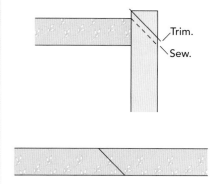

4. Fold and press the binding lengthwise, wrong sides together.

5. With raw edges even, pin the binding to the edge of the quilt, starting a few inches from the corner and leaving the first few inches of the binding unattached. Start sewing, using a $1/4''$ seam. For pucker-free bindings, use a walking foot or even-feed feature. Adjust the needle position to achieve the desired seam allowance.

6. Stop $1/4''$ from the first corner and backstitch one stitch.

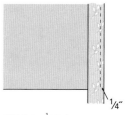

Stitch to $1/4''$ from corner.

7. Lift the presser foot and needle. Rotate the quilt one-quarter turn. Fold the binding up at a right angle so it extends straight above the quilt and forms a 45° fold in the corner.

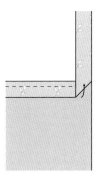

8. Bring the binding strip down even with the next edge of the quilt. Begin sewing at the folded edge. Stop ¼″ from the next corner and backstitch one stitch.

9. Repeat in the same manner at all corners. Stop sewing several inches from where you started stitching the binding to the quilt.

10. Join the ends of the binding by folding the ending binding tail back on itself where it meets the beginning of the binding. From the fold, measure and mark the cut width (2⅛″) of your binding strip. Cut the ending binding tail to this measurement.

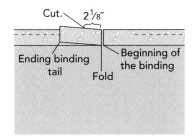

11. Open both tails. Place one tail on top of the other at a right angle, right sides together. Mark a diagonal line and stitch on the line. Trim the seam allowance to ¼″.

Press the seam open. Refold the binding strip and finish stitching it to the quilt.

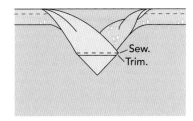

12. Turn the folded edge of the binding over the raw edge of the quilt and slipstitch the binding to the backing. Form miters at the corners.

quilt label

I always encourage quiltmakers to label their quilts. The information you include will be treasured for generations to come. Use a permanent fabric pen on the back (or even on the front) of the quilt, or design a beautiful patch specifically for the quilt with embroidery or colorful fabric pens. Before sewing the label to the quilt, consider also writing directly on the quilt (in the area that the label will cover) to ensure that the information will not be lost if the label is removed.

Label from *Cinnamon Toast* (page 29)

resources

recommended reading

Fabric and Supplies

Cotton Patch

1025 Brown Avenue

Lafayette, CA 94549

Phone: (800) 835–4418

or (925) 283–7883

cottonpa@aol.com

www.quiltusa.com

Bernina (of America)

3702 Prairie Lake Ct.

Aurora, IL 60504

Phone: (630) 978-2500

Fax: (630) 978-8214

questions@berninausa.com

www.bernina.com

Superior Threads

PO Box 1672

St. George, UT 84771

Phone: (800) 499-1777

Fax: (435) 628-6385

info@superiorthreads.com

www.superiorthreads.com

Note: Fabric manufacturers discontinue fabrics regularly. Exact fabrics shown may no longer be available.

Anderson, Alex, *Beautifully Quilted with Alex Anderson*, C&T Publishing: Lafayette, CA, 2002

———, *Hand Appliqué with Alex Anderson*, C&T Publishing: Lafayette, CA, 2001

———, *Rotary Cutting with Alex Anderson*, C&T Publishing: Lafayette, CA, 1999

———, *Machine Quilting with Alex Anderson*, C&T Publishing: Lafayette, CA, 2007

Duke, Dennis and Harding, Deborah (editors), *America's Glorious Quilts*, Crown Publishers, Inc.: New York, NY, 1987

McClun, Diana and Nownes, Laura, *Quilts! Quilts!! Quilts!!! The Complete Guide to Quiltmaking*, 2nd edition, McGraw-Hill: New York, NY, 1998

about the author

Alex Anderson's love affair with quiltmaking began in 1978, when she completed her *Grandmother's Flower Garden* quilt as part of her work toward a degree in art at San Francisco State University. Over the years, her focus has rested on understanding fabric relationships and on an intense appreciation for traditional quilting surface design and star quilts.

For eleven years, Alex hosted television's premier quilt show *Simply Quilts* and is a spokesperson for Bernina of America. Her quilts have appeared in numerous magazines, often in articles devoted specifically to her work.

Alex has two children and lives in Northern California with her husband, a new kitty, and the challenges of feeding various forms of wildlife in her backyard. Visit her website at alexandersonquilts.com.

other books by Alex:

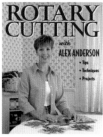

Great Titles
from C&T PUBLISHING

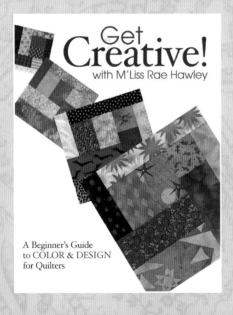